My Story

Don't Argue with God

SHERRY LYNN COOK

WESTBOW
PRESS®
A DIVISION OF THOMAS NELSON
& ZONDERVAN

WestBow Press books may be ordered through
booksellers or by contacting:

WestBow Press
A Division of Thomas Nelson & Zondervan
1663 Liberty Drive
Bloomington, IN 47403
www.westbowpress.com
844-714-3454

ISBN: 978-1-6642-2480-3 (sc)
ISBN: 978-1-6642-2481-0 (e)

Library of Congress Control Number: 2021903603

Print information available on the last page.

WestBow Press rev. date: 03/24/2021

I dedicate this story to all my loved ones who have preceded me to heaven. Each one has loved, taught, and influenced me in some way to help me through life's trials. I know that missing them in my life now is only a temporary situation. I know I will one day be with them again and say, "Wow, what a reunion!"

Introduction

Well, here I sit, sixty-two years old, retired, and with a little time on my hands—not much but a breather. I decided after all these years of endless running to finally jot down, or try to at least, an account on paper of my firsthand experiences for those who may want to share it with me. I am definitely not a writer, so bear with me.

Maybe I'll mention just a little about myself. I am a mother of an adult daughter, two grandsons, and an adult son. I am a creative person, which means I am always working on some type of craft project. I am ridiculously organized, which drives most of my family quite crazy. I love my gardens except when it is so hot outside. I am grateful to have a close and supportive family. I am remarried in my second marriage. I am still sad that my first marriage did not survive the pressures of life and being young.

I have a half sister five years older than me, four brothers younger stairstepping downward approximately two years between each one, numerous in-laws, and extended family. And naturally, with parents who pushed responsibility on me 24/7, I am pretty bossy. I have some pretty great friends. I try to avoid anyone else's self-imposed drama. I consider myself to be dependable, honest, and loyal—and yes, I was a Girl Scout. In spite of all my efforts, I do have my bad days like everyone else.

Why now, after thirty-eight years, do I want to record this? Before I die, I want to make sure my family and friends look at life a little gentler and believe that God and heaven are real. I want them to know I love them and will always be there for them.

I ask myself, Should I record this? In this year of political upheaval, riots, and COVID-19, why not? Maybe some good may come to someone reading this— at least I hope so.

Prologue

At the time this story began, I was twenty years old and had been married for a little less than two years. We both came from large, close-knit families. At this point in time, I was not working a full-time job because we were down to only one vehicle. Our income level was below moderate, to say the least, but we did as well as most newlywed couples. Sometimes when looking back, I wonder how we did it all. Part of me still misses those times even with the hardships. Sometimes you cannot see the forest because of the trees, or so I have been told.

My husband and I had purchased our first starter home about thirty-five miles outside the city of Henderson. It was a tiny little block home, and we thought we were all set for our future. It was time to start what was expected. It was time to start a family of our own. We did not really think that one through.

CHAPTER 1

My Escort

By all accounts from my doctors, not only should I not be here by medical standards, but I should not expect to live to see old age. This story goes back to 1982. Though some things from that time period may be a little dimmer, this occurrence is still quite vivid, as if it happened yesterday.

By the end of 1981, we learned that I was expecting our second child. At first, I mostly dealt with the typical morning sickness, though it lasted all day long. I had the same symptoms as my previous pregnancy with our daughter in 1978. She was born through a vaginal delivery after only three and a half hours of labor in March 1979, weighing eight pounds and ten ounces. The only issue was that I was given Demerol for pain, only to find out it was not a drug I ever wanted to take again. Anyway, healthy baby, happy family.

I have always believed in the existence of God, Jesus, and guardian angels. I attended various churches from time to time throughout my lifetime but never stayed committed for more than a few months at a time. I was christened (Baptist) as a baby and saved when I was in grade school, but I still do not view myself as the perfect Christian. I do not consider myself to be a bad person either.

Anyway, getting back to 1982. As my pregnancy progressed from three months into term, I only weighed 106 pounds, and I am a little less than five feet, five inches tall. At six months, I noticed the first signs of breast milk coming in, and morning sickness was long over—thank God! At seven months, I began to notice tiny red dots on my skin. I learned much later that they were called petechiae. I showed this to the doctor, and he did not seem concerned. The second thing I noticed was that my milk production ceased. The doctor was not concerned about this either. By the end of the ninth month, I weighed in at a healthy 168 pounds. Well, maybe not so healthy because I was having spontaneous nosebleeds (real gushers) for no reason. Again, the doctor was not concerned about this. Looking back, I realized the doctor did not seem concerned about very much with me.

July 2, 1982, I noticed the typical mommy pressure on the bladder while alternating between household tasks and going to pee. Family was coming to town for a Fourth of July celebration, so I wanted to make sure the house was clean. It was pretty aggravating trying to sweep and mop the floors with a bandana tied under my nose because blood was dripping everywhere. I felt all right. The doctor was not concerned even though my June 30 due date had passed. The holiday came and went with no issues, just peeing often and making sure the nursery was all set up. Thankfully, the nursery was not gender specific.

On July 6, 1982, my aunt and uncle had invited my husband and me to lunch because we had to drive to town for my scheduled office visit. I noticed that morning that I was going to pee even more than usual, but I felt good. We left our daughter with my aunt and uncle while I made what was supposed to be a quick trip to the ob-gyn, where the doctor promptly informed me that I was in labor and probably had been for the last four days. So, the hospital was the next stop—forget lunch.

Expecting moms typically spend a good portion of their time preparing for the new addition to the family, but I just assumed this baby was a girl too. I do not know why I thought this looking back because no test had been done. Back then, ultrasounds were not just automatically done. It was a wait-and-see game. I had little baby girl clothes (mostly left from our daughter), I crocheted a baby girl blanket and sweater set, and I had a girl's name picked out. We had purchased a new baby doll for our first daughter with matching outfits and blankets, so when I came home from the hospital, our daughter and I would have matching babies. We thought this may help with any jealousy issues.

Inside the maternity ward, I signed the usual admitting paperwork, prepared myself with the fashionable hospital gown, and waited for the doctor to show. Still no labor pain yet. I noticed in the cubicle across from me was a young lady (approximately my age, around twenty-four) in hard labor, and she had been for the past thirteen hours according to the nurse. My doctor finally came in for my exam and to break my water. Then it happened.

The doctor backed away from me with his skin as pale as the white coat he was wearing. The doctor never said a word to me, but I heard him tell the nurse to get me to delivery. This was when I felt my first labor pain. It wasn't a bad contraction, not backbreaking labor like

I had with our daughter. I thought, *This is good. I can do this.* After the Demerol experience, I was determined to have *no* drugs. I then heard the poor woman across from me scream as another hard labor pain hit. I remember asking the nurse to take her first because I was doing so well, or so I thought. The nurse only nodded her head and smiled at me.

Down in delivery with contractions coming faster and harder, I barely paid any attention to anyone or anything around me. The pain was now excruciating. The doctor told me to bear down and push hard. I was thinking, *Wow, this is fast.* I remember sitting up to push with all I had. I felt weak and fell back on the table. Then there was no pain. I knew I was fully conscious, but at the same time, I could not move any part of my body, speak, or open my eyes.

It seemed like a lifetime passed through my mind all in a microsecond. I thought of my husband, our little girl, my mom and dad, and my brothers. I knew they would miss me. I knew I would miss them. Really? What kind of mom would want to leave her child? I made peace, knowing I loved them and knowing they would be OK in life without me because they would lean on one another and help one another. I knew they would not forget me. I was ready to go. I felt so light. I heard the doctor call code blue. I heard a nurse retrieve a shock cart from the hall just outside the swinging doors behind me. I heard the doctor call for my blood (type A negative) and heard a response that they were out of my blood type. He said he did not care. He said he would give me what they had and worry about it later. Up to this point, I had been given no drugs.

Then I could see. I was looking down on my own body—the people in the room, what they were doing, the instruments on the tables, and the shock cart beside my body not yet used. I was curious but not afraid. I was floating over my body's left shoulder. I turned my spirit to the upward left to see a white light. The light was very bright and beautiful but did not hurt my eyes. It was a light like nothing I had ever seen here on earth. Suddenly, there was calmness. I do not mean a calm from the doctors and nurses (that was a beehive of activity) but around my spirit.

There appearing right in front of me was my deceased great-grandmother. She was dressed in a long white gown with long sleeves. Her gown seemed to have a sort of iridescence. I never knew white had a color, not like that anyway. Her hair was long and still pulled up in a loose bun, but it was blonde and thicker than when she passed away. I remember her having only gray hair since I was a toddler. A light made a complete circle behind her whole body in a halo-type effect. She was smiling. She was beautiful. She was appearing to me in a much younger age than when she died at 102, but she was old enough for me to recognize her. She was now the young, beautiful, intelligent, and healthy lady she had been in her prime. Do not ask why or how I know this. It was simply placed in my mind. She spoke to me through her thoughts. She simply stood still with her hands clasped in front of her.

To the right of where my great-grandmother was standing was a large gathering of people I knew who were deceased. I knew they were there, but I could not see them. I had the distinct feeling that I was not meant to see beyond. For the first time in my life, I felt nothing negative—no pain, no sorrow or loss, no worry or stress, and no anger or hate. Everything negative was gone. I knew then that only the good and positive goes with you when you die. Up to this point in my life, I had always feared death and dying. I no longer had any fear.

I knew my great-grandmother had been sent to be my escort. I wanted to go to her and hug her. I remember her smile was deep, loving, happy, and pure. I spoke to her, wondering why she did not reach out to me. She spoke to me, not with her lips but with our minds. She said, "I am waiting for permission."

Permission? I wondered.

She smiled and nodded her head to someone over my left shoulder. I turned to see a figure of a man. A sense of power came from this figure like I had never felt from anyone before. His hair was kind of shoulder-length, long, and dark. I thought how strong and handsome he was. He did not introduce himself.

He told me, "No. Now is not your time. You will go back to raise your *son*. He will have blond hair and blue eyes. He will be perfectly healthy."

I did not want to return, especially after feeling what it was like to carry only the good feelings. Really? I would give up my son too? I started to argue with this powerful man that I wanted to go with my great-grandmother.

He replied, "*No*. Now is not your time."

I felt a multitude of power and authority and knew, and I was afraid to argue with this man.

Suddenly, I was back in my body. I opened my eyes. I could move. The pain was excruciating once more. It had been less than four minutes.

The doctor yelled at the nurse, "Get her to OR."

My husband was at the nurses' station outside the swinging doors. I saw the doctor shove some papers into his chest as he said, "Here, sign these. We almost lost her."

I did not get to speak to my husband, only to see how pale his face was. I felt sorry for him after seeing the look on his face. Then into the elevators I went.

Up to this point, I still had no drugs in my system. I had only the standard fluid IV. In the OR, I was given blood and put under for a caesarean section. Two days later, I woke up in the isolation ward. I could remember every single detail of what had happened and knew I had a son. I had been given numerous units of blood and platelets. My platelet count had dropped to three thousand at one point. What was a blood platelet, and what should the count be anyway? Actually, I found out later it should have been in the three hundred thousand range.

I saw a nurse pass by the hall window in my room. I was alone, so I found the call button next to my hand. I remembered everything and wanted to see our son for the first time. The nurse brought our baby in: eight pounds, eleven ounces with blond hair and blue eyes. He was healthy. He was beautiful. I only had enough strength to hold him for a few minutes, but my heart will hold him for eternity.

On the evening of the day I woke up, my husband came to see me. Being in isolation, I was only allowed a handful of people closest to me to visit. Everyone coming in had to be dressed in a gown, bonnet, booties, gloves, and mask. The only thing I could see on them was their eyes. My husband had named our son to get the birth certificate going and because the medical staff had no idea how long it would be before I woke up. I did not have a boy's name (or anything else for a boy, for that matter) picked out anyway.

It seemed my son and I were both medical marvels. We both should have died. People (meaning medical staffing) started coming by to see for themselves. Word had gotten around, and so many could hardly believe we were still here. I recognized the anesthesiologist by his pretty blue eyes. I had four doctors, multiple nurses, and lab technicians.

When I told the doctor what I had seen and heard in the delivery room (code blue, call for blood, etc.), he said, "Not possible. You were dead."

The doctor told me that I was out for two days because of blood transfusion shock. I asked him what a three thousand blood platelet count meant.

Now he was in shock. "You could not possibly know that!" he said.

But I did know.

He went on to explain what happened with our son. "It seems the placenta had separated approximately 45 percent prior to birth—long before birth from the looks of it. He should have been born dead or mentally impaired at the very least. It seems as if he was living almost independently from your body. I just cannot explain it."

As far as my condition, I had developed ITP (idiopathic thrombocytopenic purpura) early in my pregnancy. The ITP made my blood so thin that hormones did not circulate and connect properly. Thus, I had no breast milk and was four days of overdue because my body could not prep properly. My skin had red freckles all over my body, and I had blood blisters in my mouth. The only reason I did not have a stroke was because the nosebleeds were relieving the pressure on my brain. My blood was literally leaking out of my veins and the pores of my skin. The medical records listed the diagnosis of lifesaving recovery as "unexplained intervention."

Our baby son was placed in with the preemie babies until the doctors could get a proper diagnosis on the both of us. He had only a minor case of jaundice and was placed under an ultraviolet light for a couple of days. He was alert and rarely cried. The nurses fell in love with him. It did look a little strange to have an eight-pound baby in among the three-, four-, and five-pound babies. He looked so huge.

So, what saved me and my baby? It's not *what* but *who—God!*

All right, let us do the math:

The average woman at approximately five feet, five inches tall at 165 pounds has about 9 pints (4,500 cc) of blood in her body.

Blood Loss Chart
15%–30%: Class 2
30%–40%: Class 3 (loss of 3-4 pints, needs transfusion)
> 40%: Class 4 (heart and organ failure/death)

1 pint of blood = 500 cc
1 unit of blood = 300 cc

I lost approximately 2,000 cc of blood (more than 40 percent). I was given one unit of packed cells and six units of platelets (2,100 cc or 4.2 pints). The blood bank was so low I was given three units of A positive, two units of O negative, and one unit of AB negative. And, of course, I was given a Rho immune globulin shot to follow all that mixture up.

Six days after I gave birth, mother and son went home, but only after I sent my husband out to purchase baby boy things. I did not want our son's newborn photos dressed in pink.

After going home, my doctors wanted me to stay home in isolation. Don't do this, don't do that, and limit visitors. After a while, I decided that you cannot live your life that way, especially raising two small children. Isolation is not living. I am smart enough to know to be careful about what I do. I also placed what I cannot control into God's hands. Well, it must be working. I am still here at the age of sixty-two and still somewhat healthy.

I also went back to college in the medical field when our son was two. It was really tough with two small children and a ton of homework every night, but I was driven to do it. Not only did I want a better paying job, but I thought maybe I could find a more scientific reason for the things I had been through. I did not, but I did graduate with honors in medical administration.

Five years after our son was born, I had a splenectomy to bring the ITP under control. I have done well. Our son continues to thrive. I wonder: Will my great-grandmother still be my escort when it is my time to go? I no longer fear death because of what I witnessed firsthand because life continues.

Something I learned from this near-death experience is that heaven is not a distance away. It is a dimension away. Heaven is so close. Think of yourself standing in a room near a doorway, and heaven is on the other side of that door. Now, all you have to do is reach through. Everyone you love is there in that world, and they have the ability to pass back and forth at any time they please. You are never truly alone. Another thing is I was somehow left with the feeling that time as we know it does not exist in heaven. I cannot explain it. It is just different somehow.

ME, DAUGHTER, SON, GREATGRANDPARENTS

Me at three months into the pregnancy with our son, weighing in at 106 pounds.

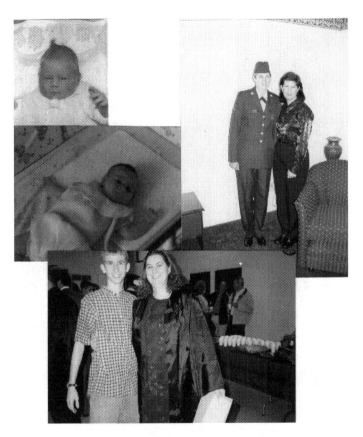

Our daughter is doing well. We are blessed with two grandsons. After her hitch in the US Army and additional college, she is a licensed practical nurse and is currently working in a nursing home.

Our son has continued to thrive through adulthood. After his hitch in the Marines and additional college, he presently works in the aviational field as a technical manual writer. He recently married the most wonderful woman.

My great grandmother married her "little redheaded Irishman" and came from Tennessee to Kentucky in a covered wagon. She was very intelligent as her father had been a school master. She was a quiet person but had spirit and spunk. She hand stitched me a quilt when I was only six years old to put away until I got married. I still have it.

CHAPTER

2

It Does Not Seem Fair

During the time of my healing and returning home with our son, a close friend of mine became ill with cancer. She had two young boys between the ages of our two children. She was a very sweet and kind person. Because of the hardships with the treatments and the recovering surgery, she, her husband, and their two boys moved in with her parents.

One afternoon, when our son was just about two months old, she called and wanted to see him. We came to visit with her (I remember it was her birthday), and she wanted to take a walk to have a little privacy. She told me she thought her cancer had returned. I asked her how she knew.

She said, "I just know." She told me it was breaking her heart knowing she would be leaving her boys. She did not want them to forget her. I told her about what happened to me when our son was born. She did not speak much. She was just quiet and thoughtful. I hope my experience was able to help her in some small way.

After she passed, her mother took me into my friend's room. She told me about the night she passed. Her father awoke to hear my friend speaking to someone. Before entering her room, he thought he saw a glowing light, a flickering like candlelight. He went into her room to find her alone and awake. He asked her who she was talking to.

She said, "My guardian angels, Daddy. Can you not see them?" She pointed to the upper corner of the room at the foot of her bed.

He told her he could not, but he believed they were there. He asked her, "Honey, are you ready to go?"

She replied, "Yes, Daddy. I am." She passed away early that morning.

As for me, I believe her. It just does not seem fair to die so young. Was I able to give her a little more than just my friendship? I hope so.

CHAPTER

3

Saying Goodbye

After my friend's passing, I thought of many stories that I grew up hearing from relatives and such. One story in particular involved a child. I think that is why the story impacted my mind and heart so much.

One afternoon while I was playing with my cousins in our grandparents' front yard, I decided to eavesdrop on the adults. So, I plumped my little girl's bottom of the edge of the concrete porch. It was evident the adults were not taking much notice of my presence. Children love to listen most when they are not supposed to.

My grandmother, her sister, my mom, and two of Mom's sisters were sitting on the front porch talking. My grandmother was recounting the time when she lost her second-born child, Geraldine. Mom was only four years old at that time in 1938 when Geraldine died, so she only remembered bits and pieces. Geraldine was only two years old and was extremely ill. I do not know what the medical diagnosis was, only that it involved high fever and chronic diarrhea.

Late one morning my grandfather was on a tractor out in the field. My grandfather was legally blind, but back then, people did whatever job they could get to put food on the table. Over the sound of the running tractor, he heard Geraldine say, "Daddy." He was sure he heard her but wondered how. What was she doing out of bed? How did she get out into the field? He was so afraid he may run over her that he shut the tractor off. He jumped down and circled the tractor to find no sight of her. He was so upset he decided to go back to the house.

Meanwhile, my grandmother told Geraldine to stay still because she had to go to the outhouse (another nonluxury of the poor farmer back then). While grandmother was taking care of business, she heard Geraldine say, "Momma." She was sure she heard her.

Grandmother said, "Geraldine, what are you doing out of bed?"

Grandmother wondered, *How did Geraldine get outside to the far back property of the house? She is too weak to walk.* Grandmother came out and circled the outhouse to find no sight of her. She was so anxious she practically ran back to the house.

Upon reaching the screen door at the back kitchen, grandmother was surprised to find granddaddy already there. She asked, "What are you doing here?"

He said, "I heard Geraldine call me."

"I heard her too."

They came inside to Geraldine's bedside to find their little baby girl had passed on.

I think this was Geraldine's way of saying goodbye. This recount from my grandmother was so unnerving and sad that it has stayed with me all these years. I wonder who this child's guardian angel was. Did Jesus Himself carry the little one to heaven like we had learned in Bible school? I would like to think so. If so, I would not be the least bit surprised.

GRANDPARENTS

Grandmother and Grandad lived in some very difficult financial times. Getting married and starting a family with only pocket change. She told me once she used wooden crates for end tables and I still have a kerosine lamp that was one of their first purchases. She taught me how to embroidery when I was in grade school.

CHAPTER

4

The Test

So, if there is heaven, does Hades exist, or at least some evil dominion?

This took place two and a half to three months after mother and son came home in early Autumn of 1982.

My husband worked the second shift, so he left the house around two thirty in the afternoon. We lived in a quiet little subdivision where neighbors knew and looked out for each other. Locking a door was not such a major issue as it is now. Like usual, I had the front door open for the warm sunshine and the clear view the glass storm door provided. It was a typical and very quiet afternoon. This occurrence was even more unbelievable by most people's way of thinking. Truly, it was unbelievable by my way of thinking too.

I had put our three-year-old daughter down for her afternoon nap in her bedroom. Our newborn son was sleeping in his nursery straight down the hallway from the living room where I was watching television. I decided to do a quick check on the baby because it was getting near his feeding time anyway.

I was doing very well, and my strength was not exactly normal (not with two babies to care for) but good.

Halfway down the hallway, I felt an ice-cold air pocket, not a breeze but a single, isolated pocket (like a bubble) behind me. I thought it was kind of weird. I did not turn around. No big deal, right? Immediately I felt there was an extreme evil behind me. My first thought was that someone had gotten into our home. I felt the evil. I know, weird. How do you feel evil? But that is as close as I can explain it. I turned around to see a cloud. It was clear, so I could see through it. It was sort of like looking underwater in a swimming pool. The clear cloud was a little taller than me but floated about one foot off the floor. It had no particular shape or form. Inside this clear cloud were tiny black specs like coarse black pepper floating around. It was just constantly moving but staying in the same spot. I felt frozen with fear from this pure evil. I could not believe what I was seeing. This could not be real. It had to be my imagination.

What do I do? I thought. *No one is home but me and my babies!*

Because my fear of dying was no longer in by personal being, my protective instincts as a mother kicked into overdrive. I became extremely angry. "How dare you to come into our home. You will not harm our children." I screamed these words as I advanced forward with clenched fists to fight this thing. Really? How do you fight a cloud? "Only God Himself is welcome in our home. Get out of here, and do not ever come back. You are not welcome here."

The evil cloud immediately vanished, and the air temperature returned to normal instantly. At first, I thought I was losing my mind. Then I laughed. I laughed at myself, thinking how glad I was that no one was around to see or hear me behave this way. I would be locked up. I thought I may be going crazy. I had to be, right?

Before I could even turn to head back to the nursery, a quiet male voice came to me. "You were being tested, and you have passed." I knew this to be true in my heart. But still, it was a very long time before I ever told my husband about this and many more years before I ever told anyone else. Who would believe any of this? Some did not, so I just kept quiet.

Even after all that had happened, I still felt our home to be safe from any other incidence, and it was. God gave me that assurance. Evil came in uninvited, but only God stayed.

Over the years, I have never heard or read of anyone having such an experience. But I do know to the very core of me this is true and actually did happen, even if there was no witness. I no longer care if people do not believe it. They will find out for themselves in their own given time.

I still am not a member of a particular church, but I do know where to find God. I still laugh at myself. Do not ever try to argue with God.

But it did not end here.

CHAPTER

5

Grandmothers Worry Like Moms

So, what happened between 1982 and 1994, you may ask? Other than me nearly dying again, absolutely nothing but ordinary day-to-day living. We went to work, took care of our home, ran errands, and had parental involvement with our children such as birthdays, school plays, ball games, etc. We slowly outgrew our little house and grew bored with our jobs, not to mention that the area where we lived had little to offer in the way of social entertainment. So, we slowly began to look at real estate and jobs. We moved out of state in 1990. It was rather tough leaving family and friends behind. It was a rather slow adjustment, but we all did pretty well.

Due to the splenectomy I'd had several years prior, I have a lower immunity to several things. Prior in 1992 and again in 1993, I had developed two different bacterial blood sepsis caused from bacteria found in the city water supply. I almost died and was in the hospital for nearly a week with the first one. Another time in 1994, I was in the hospital for another week and nearly died from an allergic reaction to a pneumonia vaccination.

August 1994. This next occurrence took place in our second home four states south. It was a nice late summer afternoon, and my husband was at work again on second shift (different job). I was washing dishes by hand, even though I had a new dishwasher, watching our children play with our white German shepherd in the backyard. Everything was quiet inside, and I felt good … happy. I had nothing in particular on my mind at the time.

My grandmother had passed away in May 1993. It hit me hard because we were so close. I knew I would miss her. Suddenly, I smelled my grandmother's perfume. I do not even know what she wore. It was a light scent, and I thought it was odd because she had not been on my mind at the time. I then felt a light pressure on my upper right arm. I looked to see the imprint of four fingertips in my skin. The pressure on my skin actually caused a visual (gray-white) color change in the pressure points as well. It felt like the exact same way she used to touch me. It was her type of a little minihug. Talk about being shook up. I felt her feelings of being very worried about me. Just as suddenly as she came, she left. All I could do was shake my head. I should not be so surprised after all the things I have witnessed in my life.

She came to me two other times soon after this. Each time, I was alone. Each time, she was worried about me. Each time, I felt the same touch and scent of her perfume. She made me smile. I was doing well, and I did not want her to worry. Although I did welcome her visits, I told her, "Grandmother, please do not worry so. I am really well and happy. All is fine, and I love you dearly. I will be OK. I promise."

I felt, not saw with my eyes, but felt her smile, and she left. I have not smelled her perfume since, but I know she is my guardian angel and is always within reach.

GRANDMOTHERS

My grandmother always had a hard life. She raised five children on her own. She was a seamstress and was very good at crafts. I still have many of the things she made for me. She also made my wedding dress. I do not ever recall seeing her angry. She was a giving person. Looking back now I wish I had done more for her than I did. I think she knew I loved her. I can not go back but I can move forward.

CHAPTER

6

Animals Are
People Too

I stated previously how I feared death as a younger person. One example was concerning a kitten my aunt had given to me when I was in elementary grade school. She was a beautiful long-haired calico. I named her Cuddles for obvious reasons.

One afternoon when I was playing with some neighborhood friends in the front yard, Cuddles ran up to me and collapsed at my feet. She had been hit by a vehicle. All I could do was run away to get my father. I just knew he could fix her. He gently picked her up and placed her in her soft bed. We all knew she was dying. Being the weak coward I was, I just walked away crying instead of being there for her. She passed away alone.

Another example was concerning a dog. He was a golden retriever/Alaskan Samoyed mix I picked from a litter of puppies when I was in the seventh grade. His name was Chunook. He gave a lifetime of joy and love to our family. He even adopted and mothered some orphaned kittens at one point. As he was fast approaching his senior years, he became ill. The decision was made to put him down. I was an adult by this time, but again, I took the coward's way out. I had someone else take him to the veterinarian. I again left something I loved to die alone. He did not deserve that.

I never went to a person's funeral as a child. The first one I went to as an adult I stayed in the far back of the room. I simply could not face what I thought was the end. I feared the unknown.

In the previous chapter, you read a comment about a white German shepherd. Her name was Gidget. We adopted her the same year I started medical school. She spent a lifetime of giving laughter, love, and protection to all of us. She simply adored children. Animals may not speak our English words, but they do have a language all their own. People just need to listen. By the time she reached her senior year, it was September 1998. I had already been educated by God at this point.

I had taken our son to the doctor that afternoon. Upon arriving home, my husband said, "Come right now to look at Gidget. I think she is dying. I think she has been holding on for you to come home."

Our son was definitely where I was at his age. He took one look at her, touched her head, and fled. He could not handle her dying. My heart was breaking, but my fear of dying was gone. I would not leave her.

I sat down and gently placed her head in my lap. She looked at me with an almost smile. I could tell she was glad to see me. She looked around in a near panic like she was searching. Her breathing was short and labored, and her tongue was hanging out. I could see how dry her mouth and nose were.

I told her, "It is OK. We are here for you now. You will be fine. Just relax and rest easy. I have you."

She began to relax and then looked me square in the eyes. It was a simple question: "Is it OK to go?"

I could feel her reluctance. She was afraid, and she did not want to leave me.

I told her, "It is all right to go. We love you. We will be here for you. You will not be alone."

She then took a slow, gentle breath; her body relaxed; and I watch her light leave her eyes.

I sat there holding her body for about ten minutes. I was thinking how grateful and blessed I was to be there for her, to see her into her next stage of life, and to hand her over to God. It is a strange feeling to have a sad and happy heart at the same time. Our family pets were more than just playthings and have taught me much over the years. Even to this day, I have regrets of not being there for Cuddles and Chunook. Animals are people too. God created them and loves them as well as us.

Do not bring regrets into your future out of stupidity and fear. You cannot go back and undo the past. You have to live with your mistakes.

GIDGET

Gidget, our beloved dog. She gave so much to all of us. We do miss her.

CHAPTER

7

Unfinished Business

Between 1994 and 2015, life again dropped to a steady hum of day-to-day normalcy. But during this time, my husband and I went through a difficult divorce. Both of us have now married again—well, not to each other.

This takes place in November 2015. In October, just prior, my father went into surgery for renal cancer. His downward spiral began immediately in postoperative recovery. He developed pneumonia with two other infections to follow and was then placed on life support. He remained in a coma for approximately four weeks. This next occurrence happened on the Tuesday prior to his death the following Monday.

On this Tuesday, I came to visit with Dad, knowing he was still in a coma with no change in his condition. After about forty-five minutes of sitting at his bedside, talking mostly to myself, I decided to go out for a bite to eat. As I was leaving his room, I felt something familiar that I cannot for the life of me explain. When I say "familiar," it is because there is no other way to explain it. It is a feeling in its own category that nothing else fits in. One would think that by now that familiar feeling would have been forgotten, but this feeling is buried down deep inside me. I cannot forget it.

Somehow, something made me stop and turn around. When I turned to look back at Dad, I could see he was awake. I went back to the side of his bed, thinking he would not be coherent. He had a tracheostomy, so I knew he would not be able to speak. As soon as I saw his eyes, I knew he was mentally awake and crystal clear with his thoughts. He smiled at me when he saw me. As I spoke to him, he followed me with his eyes, held my hand, and nodded his head to my yes/no questions. I considered this to be a positive sign on the road to his recovery.

After our short visit, I could see that he was tiring, so I told him goodbye and that I loved him. He smiled and nodded his head yes. I kissed him and told him I was leaving to get a bite to eat and that I would be right back. As I was walking out through the doorway of his room, I felt that same familiar feeling again. I turned toward Dad to see him looking out the picture window.

I could tell he was talking to someone with his thoughts. With my eyes, I could see no one. He was arguing that he had something to finish first—something he absolutely had to do. That same familiar feeling told me he was talking to his guardian angel and that I was not to interrupt. I could see his face and his anxiety, not from his fear or sadness but from his need. How do I know what he was thinking? How do I know any of this? I just do. I cannot explain it. It was just put inside me. Sometimes I wonder if some type of doorway was opened for me when our son was born.

There were two nurses in his room attending monitors and recording entries. Neither of them seemed to notice any of this. I thought this was odd. Why is there never a witness?

I left to get a bite to eat and returned about an hour later. He had slipped back into his coma. I think I knew when I left it was his time to go. I just did not want to let him go. The next night he went into seizures due to high fever, and in the days to follow, he was pronounced brain dead.

On Sunday, with my mom and brothers all gathered around Dad's bedside, I signed him off life support. My mom was pulling on my arm and screaming, "Please do not sign those papers. Please do not let them kill your daddy!"

It was one of the most difficult things I have ever had to do, even though I knew he was already gone both physically and mentally. No matter what, you always question yourself.

Mom screamed at Dad, "You promised you would not go first. I was supposed to go before you. Please do not go!"

To this very day, I always wonder what it was—that unfinished business he felt he needed to take care of. In the end, it does not matter. Do not argue with God. Some day when it is my time to move on to my next adventure of our heavenly life, maybe he will tell me.

Why is it that people always say "rest in peace"? I have seen for myself that after this earthly life is over, the best part of living is yet to come. As for me, I plan on one grand celebration and reunion party. "Rest in peace" is not in my vocabulary. Although I do not fear death and look forward to the new life, I do not wish to rush this one, because I have loved ones here too. I am not really through living here in this life just yet. I want to create more memories to take with me when I go.

DAD, PARENTS

Dad was never content to stay put in one spot. We never lived in any one place for very long. The only "home" I truly called as such we lived in for a period of five years. Maybe that is why I hate moving so much. He was terrible with financial matters but we never went hungry. He loved his family but was not really that great at conveying that. We never had much money but Christmas was always good. He handmade a life sized Nativity scene when we were kids. Now Christmas is not quite the same as it was back then. Dad was a self taught "Jack of all trades" and was very good at most things he attempted.

My parents, through thick and thin, mostly due to the patience and love from my mom I think!

CHAPTER

8

A Mother Forever

After the death of my father and after making all the funeral arrangements, I took over full guardianship of my mother. It took me well over a year to sell their estate and clear out all the legalities. She had several health issues and did not drive a vehicle. Because of her health, everyone thought she would be the first to go. It does not matter what we think or want. Do not argue with God.

I tried to make life for Mom as happy as possible, though I know she was always grieving quietly inside herself. I tried to make life for her as normal and as fulfilled as possible. I tried to keep her busy with crafts, cooking, and reading material. We always turned doctor visit days into extended shopping and restaurant adventures, which always ended with a Dairy Queen ice-cream cone (triple scoop).

I took an early retirement to take care of her increasing medical needs. Just short of three years following my father's death, Mom had to be placed in hospice care at a facility. Believe me, those people are wonderful. I tried my best to keep her at home, but her multiple needs became too much for any one person to handle.

On August 1, 2018, Mom was taken off all medications. She refused anything to eat or drink (even Dairy Queen cones). She was comfortable and alert for the first five days and had many visitors, including her little Chihuahua, Baby. She slept soundly for the next seventeen days.

I know many people have had to go through situations such as this in their lifetimes. I told everyone she would not go with me beside her. She did not like to leave me or let me out of her sight. I only lived a half of a mile from the facility, so I came home to sleep at night and to grab a quick bite to eat. I was at her side every chance I could be.

The day before she passed, she woke as I kissed her cheek. I started to cry. She frowned, put her hand on my arm, and asked me, "Are you all right?"

Here she was, lying there dying with all her multiple issues, and she still worried about me. So, of course, I just cried harder. I finally made myself regain a little control and told her that I was fine and that I loved her. She smiled and returned to a peaceful sleep once again.

How does a person go twenty-one days without food, water, or medications? Do you have any idea how hard it is to say goodbye every time you leave, not knowing if it will be the last time?

I had been sitting with Mom, holding her hand, and talking to her all morning. I do not think she really heard anything I was saying, but I felt better talking to her. Then again, who is to say she did not hear me? The only light we kept on in her room was a small lamp at the foot of her bed. If you have ever been to a hospice facility, things are kept very quiet and serene. At noon, I decided to run home for a bite to eat.

The next experience included me but was more to have been witnessed by my husband and the hospice nurse. Finally … *witnesses!*

At about one o'clock, my husband said, "I think I

would like to go with you this time. I do not think your mom will be with us much longer."

He did not want to stay all evening, so we each took separate vehicles. He was about two minutes ahead of me because of traffic. As I was turning into the parking lot, he called. He said, "Get in here now. I think she is gone."

I ran into Mom's room. As soon as I touched her, I knew she had passed. I could not feel any presence of her in that room at all. I knew she would not go with me right there with her. I knew she would wait for me to leave.

The following words are from my husband:

> I was standing at Mom's bedside, holding her hand, and she was in labored, deep breathing. Her eyes were closed. It was getting longer and longer between each breath, so I called my wife and told her to get in here now. Then I hit the nurse's call button.
>
> The nurse came in, and I told her I thought Mom was close to passing. The nurse was standing just behind my left shoulder, watching the labored breathing. Mom's mouth was wide open. All of a sudden, her mouth closed, the deep breathing stopped, and she began relaxed breathing through her nose. At the same time, she opened her eyes and looked around the room with a

total look of pure peace on her face. As her eyes opened, the entire room lit up with an amber glow that came from everywhere, but not the bedside lamp. The glow only lasted about three to four seconds and then it disappeared. As it disappeared, her eyes closed, and her breathing stopped.

At that point I asked the nurse, "Did you see that glow?"

I then turned around to look at the nurse. Her eyes were big, and she replied, "Yes, I saw that!" At that point, I asked the nurse if Mom was gone.

She listened with the stethoscope and replied, "Yes, she is gone." Then my wife came in.

For nearly four months to follow, I felt Mom at my side no matter where I went or what I was doing. Everyone said, "It is just because her things are all around you, just memories,"

No, it was more than that. Mom was worried about me—about us. I could feel it all the way through me. Her children always came first in her life. Her presence was with me all the time.

On Christmas Eve, I felt as if I were to reach out my hand, I would be able to touch her. On Christmas Day, I had dinner at my house. Mom would host almost all the holiday dinners because she absolutely loved to cook. She also wanted her children and their families together under one roof, preferably hers.

I was not sure how we would all feel because it was our first Christmas without Mom. It turned out to be the usual jovial chaos that most reunions are. After everyone had gone home, she went home too. It was almost as if she went out the door when the lasts guests left. I had to laugh because she did not even say goodbye. She was satisfied that everyone was doing well and we were still a connected family. She was finally at peace that we would be all right. As I say, "A mother forever."

I do not have any idea what the remaining portion of my life holds in store for me. Please hold your loved ones close, forgive each other the ridiculous disagreements, and be happy in this life. The next life will take care of itself.

Sherry Lynn Cook

MOM

Mom was a strong individual. I wish I could be more like her. She had a reserved personality but laughed most of the time. She always gave up material things for herself to make sure her children had what we needed. I did not realize until I grew up just how much she gave. She was very protective of her family. She was well known for her southern cooking, making and decorating cakes......part of the reason we never went hungry. She was always trying to feed someone. She could cook for an army and make it look easy. She liked working on craft projects.

CHAPTER

9

Moms Know Best

Rose Louise, "Love little Rose." An unexpected gift.

Backing up time just a little, this little story took place beginning August 1, 2018. We got up that morning with two sorrowful tasks. We had to put down our beloved little dog because of lymphatic cancer. She was a rescued beagle mix, and her name was Mia. It was the same day Mom went into the hospital.

Halfway into the month, my husband decided I needed something to help pick me up—something to bring me some happiness out of our grief. His answer was—you guessed it—a puppy. *No, no, no, no.* I was dead set against taking on another responsibility. We still had two other dogs at home, and Mom was in hospice. A few days later, he brought home a beagle puppy.

I was so angry and upset, not to mention stressing and grieving. I told him, "You wanted a dog. You will have all 100 percent responsibility of it. You will feed, bathe, clean up, and potty train all on your own. I do not want it. I want nothing at all to do with it."

I know that sounds cruel, but I just could not take on anything else. As sweet as a puppy is, they are a lot of time and work. I just did not have it in me. I was angry because my husband did not respect my wishes. From the time he brought the puppy home, I did not do anything for her. I did not even look at her or hold her.

Mom passed away on August 22. I still had not touched the puppy. My husband was taking care of her and was in the process of finding her a new home.

One afternoon during the first week of September

my husband had a routine doctor's visit. While he was gone, the puppy had gotten pretty antsy. I knew she needed to go out. Well, it looked like I would have to take care of his responsibility. I leaned down and, for the first time, gently picked the pup up out of her box. Almost immediately, I heard Mom's voice, "Love little Rose." Just three simple and clear words. I was home alone. I nearly dropped the pup. I quickly put the pup back in her box. Never mind about going out.

Roses were my mom's favorite flower. She especially loved the orange ones of her birth month flower. Roses were the planned arrangements we were hosting for her upcoming funeral service. I was a little confused. Was Mom telling me she loved the flowers chosen for her service? I had a very distinct feeling she was referring to the puppy. I just could not shake that gut feeling.

After Mom's service was over, I decided to give the puppy a chance. Well, guess whose dog she is now? Mine. Her AKC registered name is Rose Louise. "Love little Rose"—just three simple and clear words. I feel like Mom knew me better than I knew myself. I am glad now that I listened to her.

ROSE

Rose Louise "Love Little Rose" An unexpected gift.

Epilogue

There is one very odd thing about thinking back to 1982. The vision I had of God is so very clear. Every tiny detail of what happened is still so clear in my mind's vision even today. I remember thinking God was not only powerful but a very handsome man. Immediately after returning to my body, I thought it was a strange thing that I could not describe the details of his facial features. I can only remember how I loved his face. Was it meant for me not to remember his features? But why? But I feel without a doubt I will be sure to know him when I see him again.

So, you would think after occurrences such as this it would greatly change a person's life. Am I special in some way? Am I a changed person? No, I do not think so. Other than my fear of dying diminishing and my proof of God being reenforced, I am still just me. I just quietly accepted that it happened, and I am still alive. I am just a person like anyone else getting through life on a day-to-day basis, with some good days and some rough days. I set in on living my life as before, only with two children instead of one, with my husband and our family. I live every day the same as most people, trying to make the financial ends meet, trying to take at least one mini family vacation each year when possible, and having an occasional get-together with friends. I really do not think about what happened so much. I just feel safe putting our lives into God's hands. Life marches forward.

One thing I am sure of: I do know that no matter what happens, I am never truly alone.

ME AND HUSBAND

Me and my husband in March of 2020. Photo snapped at our son's wedding just a few short hours prior to the first Covid 19 shut downs.

Printed in the United States
by Baker & Taylor Publisher Services